Joe MONTANA

The Comeback Kid

Written and Illustrated by Jim Spence

THE ROURKE PRESS, INC.
VERO BEACH, FL 32964

B
Montana

Edited by Sandra A. Robinson and Pamela J.P. Schroeder

LIBRARY OF CONGRESS CATALOGING-IN-PUBLICATION DATA

Spence, Jim
   Joe Montana, the comeback kid / written and illustrated by Jim Spence.
      p. cm. — (Great comeback champions)
    ISBN 1-57103-003-4
    1. Montana, Joe, 1956-   .—Juvenile literature. 2. Football players—United
States—Biography—Juvenile literature. I. Title. II. Series: Spence, Jim. Great
comeback champions.
GV939.M59S64   1995
796.332'092—dc20
[B]   CIP

Printed in the USA

"With only seconds left to play, Montana drops back to pass. He throws the ball and ... touchdown! The 49ers win!" shouts the TV announcer.

Joe Montana's career as a quarterback has been filled with so many exciting victories, his nickname is "The Comeback Kid."

Starting Out

Joe's father helped him to do well in sports as a young boy growing up in Monongahela, Pennsylvania. He made a hoop so Joe could shoot basketballs, and hung a tire from a tree that Joe used for target practice.

Although Joe was very thin as a child, he continued to practice. His arm got stronger and his aim got better.

In high school, Joe was an excellent athlete. College scouts wanted him to play for their universities.

Working Hard

Joe took a football scholarship at the University of Notre Dame in Indiana. His first year at college was difficult. Joe's classes were challenging. He had to spend a lot of time studying.

Joe's parents had taught him the importance of getting a good education. He worked hard. He was determined to be a success not only on the football field, but also in the classroom.

As a quarterback for Notre Dame's Fighting Irish, Joe became famous for leading his team to victories with last-second touchdowns. His heroic efforts helped lead his team to the national title in 1977.

Meeting New Challenges

The next season—just when everything looked so promising—Joe suffered a shoulder injury. It would have been easy for him to give up.

However, Joe's fighting spirit would not let him quit. He began to work hard to regain his strength. By the following year, Joe was back on the field and eager to play.

In one of his most amazing comebacks ever, Joe once again led Notre Dame to victory in the 1979 Cotton Bowl. Joe felt ill early in the game and left the field. In the locker room, the team doctor noticed Joe had trouble breathing and took his temperature—it was only 96° Fahrenheit. The doctor covered Joe with blankets and fed him hot chicken soup.

Meanwhile, time was running out for the Fighting Irish. They had fallen behind 34-12. Then suddenly someone came out from the locker room—it was Joe! He came back just in time to throw three touchdown passes for another fantastic finish, a 35-34 win.

Joe graduated from college and left Notre Dame as a hero.

Turning Pro

Joe Montana began playing professional football with the San Francisco 49ers in 1979. Coach Bill Walsh had Joe practice with his fellow rookie, Dwight Clark. Dwight, a wide receiver, ran patterns while Joe threw him the ball. One day, Coach Walsh knew all their hard practice would pay off.

In only his second year, Joe had the best pass-completion record in the NFL (National Football League). By his third year, he was ready to lead his team to football's ultimate quest—the Super Bowl.

In 1981, the 49ers faced the Dallas Cowboys for the NFC (National Football Conference) championship.

With only seconds left in the game, the 49ers trailed 27-21. All eyes were on Joe as the center snapped the ball to him. The ferocious Dallas linemen came at Joe as he looked desperately for his receiver in the end zone. He threw the ball high into the air.

Someone leaped up and grabbed the ball—landing with both feet in the end zone for a touchdown. That someone was Dwight Clark! The 49ers had won the game and were on their way to the Super Bowl.

The 49ers went on to defeat the Cincinnati Bengals in Super Bowl XVI. In 1989, these two teams would meet again in perhaps the greatest Super Bowl ever played, Super Bowl XXIII.

Trailing the Bengals late in the fourth quarter, Joe Montana marched his team 92 yards down the field and threw the game-winning touchdown pass to John Taylor! Once again, the 49ers were Super Bowl Champions of the World.

Between 1982 and 1990, Joe Montana and the 49ers won a total of four Super Bowls. Joe is the only player in the history of the Super Bowl to be named Most Valuable Player three times.

Looking Back

At an age when most football players retire, Joe Montana joined the Kansas City Chiefs football team. Once again, his winning spirit helped bring his team to the playoffs.

Joe Montana gave a lot to football, and felt he got a lot in return. "I don't think anyone can really explain the feeling that takes place out on the football field. You get on the field and there's no feeling like it ... you and your teammates are on your own for those 60 minutes."

"When the game is on the line and you need someone to come through and win the big one, I'd rather have Joe in my corner than anyone else," 49ers Head Coach, Bill Walsh, believes. "He is perhaps the greatest clutch player of all time."

21

Joe MONTANA

TIMELINE AND TRIUMPHS

1956   Born June 11 in Monongahela, Pennsylvania

1967   Pitched three perfect games while batting
.500 in Little League

1971   High jumped 6 feet, 9 inches on track
team at the age of 15

1973   All-American football and All-State basketball
player in high school

1977   Won national title playing for Notre Dame

1979   Won Cotton Bowl (Notre Dame)

1982   Super Bowl XVI victory over Cincinnati Bengals
(26-21). Voted Most Valuable Player

1985   Super Bowl XIX victory over Miami Dolphins
(38-16). Voted Most Valuable Player

1989 Super Bowl XXIII victory over Cincinnati Bengals (20-16)

1990 Super Bowl XXIV victory over Denver Broncos (55-10). Voted Most Valuable Player

1990 *Sports Illustrated* Sportsman of the Year

★ Only the second quarterback to win 4 times in the history of the Super Bowl

★ Only player to have been named Most Valuable Player in Super Bowl 3 times

★ Leads top 20 passers in NFL history in completion percentage

GREAT COMEBACK CHAMPIONS

ARTHUR ASHE
Tennis Legend

BO JACKSON
Super Athlete

JOE MONTANA
The Comeback Kid

JULIE KRONE
Fearless Jockey

MUHAMMAD ALI
The Greatest

NANCY KERRIGAN
Courageous Skater